First published in the United States of America in 2008 by
dingles & company
P.O. Box 508
Sea Girt, New Jersey 08750

All rights reserved. No part of this book may be reproduced in any form without written permission from the publishers, except by a reviewer who may quote brief passages in a review to be printed in a newspaper or magazine.

First Printing

Website: www.dingles.com

E-mail: info@dingles.com

Library of Congress Catalog Card No.: 2007907143

ISBN: 978-1-59646-592-3 (library binding)
 978-1-59646-593-0 (paperback)

© Oxford University Press
This U.S. edition of *Alphabet Poems*, originally published in English in 1994, is published by arrangement with Oxford University Press.

Acknowledgments
The editor and publisher wish to thank the following who have kindly given permission for the use of copyright material:

John Foster for "Animal Alphabet", "CAPITAL LETTERS", "Alphabet Game",
all © John Foster 1994
Robin Mellor for "Snacktime ABC", originally published as "Tea-time ABC",
© Robin Mellor 1994

Illustrations by
Sarah Warburton; Karen Donelly; George Buchanan; Caroline Ewe; Sami Sweeten

Printed in China

Snacktime ABC

A is for apple pie, tasty and hot,

B is for butter, in a glass pot,

C is for crusts,
on warm bread for me,

and that is my snacktime
ABC.

Robin Mellor

Animal Alphabet

A for an *Ant*,
B for a buzzing *Bee*,
C for the *Cat*,
which climbs up the tree.

D for DANGER!
Beware of the *dog*!
E for *Elephant*,
F for *Frog*.

G for *Goat*,
H for *Hare*.
I is for me,
sitting here in this chair!

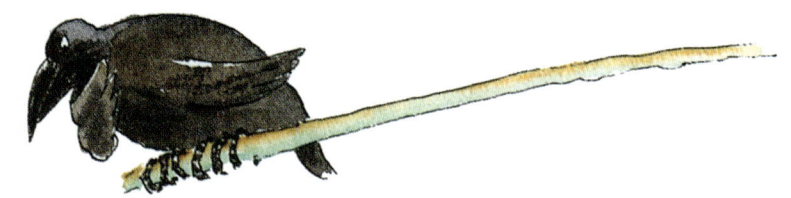

J for *Jackdaw*,
K for *Kangeroo*,
L for the *Lion*,
which is laughing at you!

M for a *Monkey*,
N for a *Newt*,
O for the *Owl*,
which gives a hoot.

P for a *Panda*,
Q for a *Quail*,
R for the *Rat*,
with its scaly tail.

S for the *Snake*,
which hisses and bites.
T for the *Tiger*,
which snarls and fights.

U for the *Unicorn*,
which lives in fairy tales.
V for *Vulture*,
W for *Whales*.

X in extinct –
things not living anymore –
as dead as the dodo
and the dinosaur.

Y for a *Yak*,
and also for *You*!
Z for the *Zebra*,
the last in our zoo.

John Foster

CAPITAL LETTERS

We are CAPITAL LETTERS. Use us at the start of names of places, like London and Glasgow, and people, like Gopal and James.

We are CAPTIAL LETTERS.
You can see us on signs around you,
like DANGER and STOP and WAIT,
and CIRCUS and FAIR and ZOO.

John Foster

Alphabet Game

I can spell *alphabet*,
as you can see.
How many words
can you make out of me?

John Foster

Number Poems

Selected by John Foster

First published in the United States of America in 2008 by
dingles & company
P.O. Box 508
Sea Girt, New Jersey 08750

All rights reserved. No part of this book may be reproduced in any form without written permission from the publishers, except by a reviewer who may quote brief passages in a review to be printed in a newspaper or magazine.

First Printing

Website: www.dingles.com

E-mail: info@dingles.com

Library of Congress Catalog Card No.: 2007907143

ISBN: 978-1-59646-592-3 (library binding)
978-1-59646-593-0 (paperback)

© Oxford University Press
This U.S. edition of *Number Poems*, originally published in English in 1994, is published by arrangement with Oxford University Press.

Acknowledgments
The editor and publisher wish to thank the following who have kindly given permission for the use of copyright material:

Eric Finney for "My Best Number", © Eric Finney 1994
John Foster for "Zoo Dream" and "In Bed Again", both © John Foster 1994
Ian Larmont for "Woof", © Ian Larmont 1994
Charles Thomson for "How Many?" and "Shopping Basket,"
both © Charles Thomson 1994

Illustrations by
Sue Coney; Amelia Rosato; Caroline Crossland; Merida Woodford;
Fiona Dunbar; Jon Higham

Printed in China

Woof

One, two,
how do you do?

Three, four,
lie on the floor.

Nine, ten, let's do it again.

Ian Larmont

How Many?

How many ears has a rabbit?
How many tails has a dog?
How many feet has a baby?
How many eyes has a frog?

How many sides has a triangle?
How many sides has a square?
How many legs has a donkey?
How many legs has a chair?

How many wheels has a truck?
How many wheels has a bike?
How many friends do you have?
How many sweets do you like?

Charles Thomson

Zoo Dream

I dreamed I went
to the zoo one day.
All the animals
came out to play.
There were

ten whales whistling,
nine hippos hopping,
eight monkeys marching,
seven lions laughing,

six snakes skipping,
five donkeys dancing,
four crocodiles clapping,

three rhinos roaring,
two giraffes giggling,
and one seal snoring!

John Foster

My Best Number

Six is my best number,
and I will tell you why:
My name has got six letters—
F – R – A – N – K – Y.

Six people live in our house—
Mom, Dad, three kids, and Gran.
My stick insect has six legs,
and six is how old I am.

Eric Finney

In Bed Again

One, two, three, four!
Lost my temper,
slammed the door.

Five, six, seven, eight!
Licked the gravy
from my plate.

Nine, ten!
In bed again!

John Foster

Shopping Basket

I bought two loaves of bread.
I bought one piece of meat.
I bought three big, green apples.
I bought one sticky sweet.
I bought one custard pie.
How many things did I buy?

Charles Thomson